RESPECT FOR THE MONEY: PRINCIPLES ATTITUDES TOWARD MONEY

by Daniel P. Richardson

www.meryko-p.com

I0472522

All rights reserved. No part of this publication may be reproduced, distributed, or transmitted in any form or by any means, including photocopying, recording, or other electronic or mechanical methods, without the prior written permission of the publisher, except in the case of brief quotations embodied in critical reviews and certain other noncommercial uses permitted by copyright law. For permission requests, write to the publisher, addressed "Attention: Permissions Coordinator," at the address below.

Disclaimer and Terms of Use: Effort has been made to ensure that the information in this book is accurate and complete, however, the author and the publisher do not warrant the accuracy of the information, text and graphics contained within the book due to the rapidly changing nature of science, research, known and unknown facts and internet. The Author and the publisher do not hold any responsibility for errors, omissions or contrary interpretation of the subject matter herein. This book is presented solely for motivational and informational purposes only.

Info@meryko-p.com

Copyright © 2016 by Daniel P. Richardson

Thank you for buying my book! I hope you get a lot of good stuff out of it.

I wanted to show my appreciation that you support my work so I've put together a free gift for you.

GET YOUR GIFT!

Just visit the link above to download it now.

I know you will love this gift.

Thanks readers for reviewing my book!

Table Of Content

Principle 1. Money is like an account. It should be considered and treated with respect, not carelessly. 6

Principle 2. Do not be greedy, do not be afraid to give them out. 19

Principle 3. Do not be afraid to carry a large sum in your pocket 24

Principle 4. Think of the money as possibilities 27

Principle 5. If a problem can be solved with money - it's not a problem, it is expenses. 32

Principle 6. Do not keep the money. If it is destined to leave, it will leave. 36

Principle 7. Money is an energy. 43

Principle 1. Money is like an account. It should be considered and treated with respect, not carelessly.

Money is any verifiable or generally accepted item which is recognized as an object of exchange of goods and services between involved parties. It is a term used to describe any item that is regarded a medium of exchange, a measure of value, a standard of deferred payment or a store of value. As a medium of exchange, money can serve as an intermediary in the exchange of goods and services. Money can also serve as a standard measure of the market value of certain transactions. It can also be accepted as a means to settle owed debts. Ultimately, money should be any object which can be stored for usage, though this fact might arguably be affected by inflation.

Money can be of different types depending on the form they take. Commodity money is a term which is used to refer to all forms of commodities ranging from precious and rare metals, to different types of food like salt and rice. Representative money is an item that can be used as payment with a fixed relation to a particular commodity. Fiat money is any item that has been declared by law a legal tender. It is the physically represented form of currency usually in the form of paper or coins. It can be replaced if damaged or lost. Demand deposits are claims against financial institutions, which serve as a means to purchase goods and services. They are usually in the form of cheques or bank drafts. Electronic money is a relatively new concept which was introduced in the 21st century. Bitcoins are the most popular forms of electronic money.

Irrespective of the form money takes, it is undeniable that it has a very important value in the day to day activities of mankind. Money might be considered as one of the essential commodities of human life. It might not be as important as air, food and water, but it is definitely a very close comparison. Insufficient funds can serve as a hindrance to the development of laid out plans or potential projects. In the absence of funds, trade is practically impossible at all levels of human interaction and government.

Money as an account is a very important determinant in all forms of human interaction. It is the amount of money you have available to you both in the bank and cash at hand. It might also be the bitcoins with which you conduct online transactions or the precious metals or stones you have in your possession. No matter the form it comes in, it has the same level of vitality. It determines the way you live your life, the friends you make, your social class, the projects you embark on, your schedule and even your feeding habit. It is safe to say that it serves as a catalyst that determines the rate at which your life progresses or regresses.

Catalysts are substances which are introduced into a chemical reaction to shift equilibrium towards achieving a desired result faster or more efficiently. It is safe to say that money is a catalyst in the life every individual. Its effect can never be underestimated, because in its absence everything seems to be stagnant. Judging from this, one should always strive to achieve his financial goals by using means available to him. You should manage, spend and invest your money in lucrative ventures. You should treat what you have no matter how small or large it might seem, with respect.

At a very young age we were taught how to count and save money, but most of us failed to grab the necessary foundations of financial management. These rules are quite simple and have barely changed through the course of time. Know what you have, what you want and what you need. In order to avoid spending the limited resources available to you on things that are unnecessary, you need to get a plan on spending. This is called a budget. A budget is like a plan which outlines the funds available to you within a particular period of time. It is generally the amount of money you allocate to a particular project and the summary of what you intend on spending in other to realize them.

A budget helps both individuals and establishments to control the resources available to them. To evaluate the financial performance as regards the ever-changing economic system. This goes a long way in trying to help you keep a check on whatever you are spending or earning. In the absence of a budget, one might find himself in very serious financial troubles. The amount of money one might think was more than enough if not spent carefully might end up not being as large as he expected. This might be as a result of carelessness or a care-free attitude which comes with abundance of funds and is a consequence of poor planning. You can make a budget by yourself or you can make use the services of a financial expert. You can also use online applications to monitor your income and spending. The important thing is to keep track of the flow of your cash

Being careless with money can often lead to very undesirable situations, like being in debt or abandoning a project halfway. One should ensure he does not spend more money than he earns. Even the laws of Physics state that action and reaction are equal and opposite. You should spend according to how you earn and only on things that are necessary. Even if you spend exactly as much as you earn, you will not have enough money to cater for yourself during emergencies or unforeseen circumstances. These events, although not planned for, are inevitable throughout the course of one's life.

For instance, if your annual income is 10 000 Dollars and you spend 11 000, you end up being in debt which will surely make your life miserable. Apart from that, you would be entering the next economic year with a deficit of 1000 Dollars which is an obvious disadvantage. It is never good to start a new financial year with unpaid debts. It is obvious that being in debt, you cannot pay for the unforeseen circumstances, which might lead you to more debts. Even if you spend exactly what you earn, you might still end up in debt. The best way to avoid this is to prepare for the future and be ready to deal with the inevitable crises that might come your way.

Irrespective of the fact that the future is uncertain, planning for the future is a very good way of 'playing it safe' in a very unpredictable world. If you want to buy something in installments, you have to first consider the coming months or weeks and the projects you have lined up. If buying the item does not favor you financially, you should consider leaving it. Some activities that might bring you joy at present might be the source of your sorrow in the future if care is not taken. You can also start by establishing an emergency fund which would cater for things of this nature.

Your money can grow while you sleep if you have good use for it. One should always consider making investments. You should also be careful when choosing what investment opportunities, to avoid being defrauded. Playing it safe by placing all you have in the bank is a good idea, but it is better to invest them into something. Investments can be of different forms. You might decide to buy shares, or invest in a growing business. It is also possible to invest in oneself, by gathering new skills which might help you earn more. There are many things to consider while making investments to avoid self-inflicted misfortune. There are good as well as bad investments depending on the results.

Before putting your money into any kind of investment, you should make out time to get to know what is really about. Acting based on a friend's advice is not really a very good idea. If you are unfamiliar with the way the financial system works, do not be shy to ask questions in order to determine what risks you can handle. If the information you are provided with is vague, it is always better to play it safe by walking away if you cannot afford the services of a trained expert. You should try to get accustomed with basic terms like front and back end load, expense ratio, advisory fee, transaction fee and custodian fee.

A front-end load is like a commission you have to pay. Its net worth is then determined by subtracting the value from what you have paid. A back-end load or surrender charge is the fee charged when you sell your fund. The fee decreases yearly. A transaction fee is the amount you pay each time an order is placed to buy or sell a stock. If you consider all these variables and they are favourable to you, then you can go ahead to invest. Otherwise, it is always better to politely decline and continue looking for more favourable conditions. There are no ideal investments you just have to choose what best suits your budget. Generally, when in doubt take a walk.

There are other forms of bad investments which might not involve a third party like marriage. Couples usually make investments jointly and in the event of a divorce, they have to pay a higher surrender charge or just stay invested together for another six years. If you decide to buy a piece of property like a new house, you have to consider the value to know whether it is depreciating. Another good way to invest is to diversify. Do not put all your eggs in one basket. Investment is like gambling, if you bet all your chips at once, you might win, but if you lose you are going to lose everything. Put your money into different verified asset classes and investment sectors.

Gambling is wagering on the outcome of a certain event or activity which is wholly dependent of the theory of probability and principles of permutations and combinations. The outcomes are largely dependent on luck and chance unless you have psychic ability. The skill of the 'player' rarely comes into play. Betting is also a form of legal gambling which is mostly used in sports. What they have in common is that they both involve risks which are based only on chance and luck. This is a very bad idea in relation to money. Besides the fact that gambling can be addictive, it might even lead one into incurring huge debts and eventually bodily harm. The money used for gambling would be put in better use if it is used for other forms of investments or might even be saved up as emergency funds.

In this generation of computers and information, people tend to emulate the kind of lives they usually see on television or other means of social media. Everyone wants to look and live like the celebrities they see on Facebook or Instagram. Don't get me wrong, it is good to enjoy the frivolities of life but one has to consider a lot before opening their wallets to pay for something. Take for instance, a celebrity who earns 100 000 dollars per month, to them buying a watch for 5000 dollars is nothing. An individual with a monthly earning of 10 000 dollars might afford to buy such a luxury but it is a bad idea. For someone who earns 6000 dollars or less to do such, it is a massive and unnecessary risk. You might buy it in other to sell later, but the rate might depreciate by the time you want to sell it. Moreover, there is no guarantee that someone would want to buy it second-hand. Those that might buy would want it twice as cheap. The watch might get stolen or damaged along the line. The amount you spend for repairs is also an extra expense which might have been avoided. In the end, you find out that it wasn't a very good idea to buy the watch.

When faced with different options of something to purchase, you should always take time to consider the item that would guarantee optimal productivity. Rather than getting something just for the sake of having it, you should try to limit your spending to the barest minimum. Why buy a cup for 10 dollars if you can buy three more in another shop for the same amount? This does not entail that one should be frugal. You should spend your money and use them to make your life comfortable but at the same time, one has to be wary and consider the future. If you eat all the yams in the barn today, tomorrow you will die of hunger.

Due to the unpredictable nature of the financial institution, people are usually skeptical when it comes to spending their money. They make excuses not to spend by claiming not to have enough to spare. They also claim that spending is only for the rich and those who are economically buoyant. This statement is true but to an extent. Playing safe is not always the best way to go about when it comes to dealing with money. If you are scared of striking the ball, you will never score a goal. If are not ready to part with the money you have, you will find it difficult to gain more.

Parting with money does not mean wasting money on fruitless ventures or reckless spending like I said earlier. It means spending money on things that would make it possible for you to get more money. It might also involve investing in yourself or projects that might cost a bit. Everything should be well evaluated. The risks should be considered and calculated in order to ensure that the plan is feasible.

Money in a bank savings account is usually safe, but for the sake of adventure and search for greener pastures, one should consider putting it into use. The rich men in the society did not get to where they are by playing it safe, rather they took calculated risks to their own credit. Remember the parable about the servants to whom the master gave money and left on a journey? He came back to find that one had spent all, the other had buried the cash while the third had used the money for business and made double of what he was given. It is no surprise that he was pleased with the latter and the other was punished. The servant who buried the money was safe but he did not gain anything because the master took the money from him and he was left with what he started with

– nothing. The last servant that took advantage of the situation made extra money and was equally rewarded.

It is good to want more, but the means by which we might go about it might be wrong. Greed is a bad trait in a moral sense, but some economists might say it is a formula for economic success. The truth is that greed is usually a source of economic disaster. If you are ready to do anything to get an extra payday, then there is a very great possibility that you might run into very serious problems in the course of your career. You should be content with what you have but at the same time strive to move up the economic ladder.

If you do not buy the ticket, you can never win the lottery. If you are not ready to part with your money, you will not make more. You just have to find projects to invest in. Do not get comfortable in any position you find yourself in. Always aim higher. There are different ways of making more money from the one you already have. Investments which I have already discussed, projects, self-improvement. You can engage in projects apart from your regular job. For example, one can design a website for absolutely anything or design an app. People who have artistic skill can invest in their talent. This takes a lot of time and money but if it succeeds, it ensures that one can make extra cash to complement the regular income.

You can also get a better education or pay to acquire extra skills. This is self-improvement. This might not be a guarantee of an increase in income but it goes a long way if one is looking to earn more in the near future. If you already have a project you are working on, like photography, design or art, you might want to publicize it which obviously costs a lot. The results you get are proportional to the effort you put in rather than the effort you 'don't put in'. This process might actually help you be assured of financial security in any event of economy recession.

Principle 3. Do not be afraid to carry a large sum in your pocket

Most people are afraid to carry cash on themselves while moving around. This might be due to some security problems or simply the fear of spending too much. People usually prefer to carry their cash on credit cards in order to ensure safety and due to the fact, that it is less cumbersome to carry. This is in fact true. Money can get lost or stolen. Nevertheless, it is a risk worth taking because the advantages of traveling with cash outweigh the disadvantages.

If you are finding it difficult to curtail your spending, then you have to consider traveling without your credit card. You have to make a spending budget in order not to overstep your bounds. You have to spend on things that are within your budget. Just by looking at your wallet, you would get a rough estimate of what you have left before making any decision. If you want to buy a dress for 50 dollars and you see only 35 dollars in your wallet, this will serve as a deterrent to you. On the hand, if you have a credit card with you, you can buy the dress but you will end up being in debt. The receipts you get from the purchase can help you keep track of your spending.

Credit card malfunction can leave one stranded and might even lead to public embarrassment. Retailers can gain access to personal information such as address, spending habits and email accounts, with which they can monitor consumers for future sales. Cash transactions helps you cover your digital footprint and protect you from digital criminals like credit card fraudsters. In the event of damage or loss of your credit card, the process of replacement is usually stressful. Some establishments like hotels and car rental agencies in some countries only accept cash payments.

Your personal details are not actually secure as your credit card companies usually promise. Some might sell your information for money to a third party. This is a very disturbing fact for those that value their privacy. This information falling into the hands of the wrong people might bring one to harm. The endless messages and constant reminders and alerts they send whenever you make a withdrawal might be a source of distraction. This can be avoided by using cash for transactions and saving the receipts for further assessment.

Principle 4. Think of the money as possibilities

Money is a source of motivation to individuals to perform a task or embark on an adventure. The presence of money can serve as an incentive to work which might be formed as a result of social interaction. In modern society, economic prosperity is often regarded as a measure of individual or collective success. It is related to social esteem and stratification. Some people just simply relish the respect that comes as recognition of their hard work. Man, being a socially conscious animal would do everything within his power to move up the ladder for as little as just to have the bragging rights in their circle of friends.

People often say that money is not everything. In fact, money is not everything, but it is the only way one can come close to having everything. When you have money to spend, you are open to a world of unlimited possibilities which might remain unknown to someone who is less financially endowed. The mere psychological effect of waking up in the morning and knowing that your life is in order financially is already a huge boost to your morale and confidence in going about your duties for the rest of the day.

When you attain financial stability, every other thing seems to follow suit. Money is like a fuel used to power the engine called life. When the fuel runs low, other parts of the engine would start to malfunction and this might affect the machine as a whole. Money is there to help you fulfill your basic needs. It is the means to an end. Money is not the most important thing in life, rather it serves as a complementary factor to all the other essential factors. Money does not give you a sense of fulfillment; rather it helps you attain a fulfilled life. Happiness as a state of mind can be achieved when you have the means to fulfill your heart desire. Good education is not free and clean water is a rare commodity in some countries of the world. Most people are stuck where they are because they don't have the funds required to make a change. These people are usually unhappy but cannot do anything to alleviate the situation they find themselves in.

In the absence of money, one cannot attend to the basic needs of life like food, water, shelter and clothing. If you cannot fulfill your most basic needs, what then can you do? It is very difficult to stay happy on an empty stomach. It is impossible to be fulfilled if you are running around naked. If you do not have a roof over your head, it is actually difficult to be productive in any sphere of life. The absence of these items might lead someone into the temptation of contemplating on committing a crime in other to make ends meet. This might lead one to harboring unhealthy thoughts and showcasing a hostile behavior as a way of showing his frustration towards society. They tend to blame the 'rich' for their misfortune.

Contrary to popular belief, greed rather than money is the root of all evil. Everything in life has its own unique monetary value. Money can boost your self-belief. Money gives you authority and confidence to embark on any task you might have set out to complete. Money can 'buy' you good health. All the activities you engage in during your leisure, like going to the gym or travelling are facilitated by money. If the funds were not available, you would not be able to engage in such activities. Good quality education is not free irrespective of the fact that you are paying or that you are on a scholarship. You can afford to give your children the best and as such help them secure a better future in a cruel and competitive economic system.

When your finances are in shambles, no one would want to come close to you. People would be of the belief that you are just hanging around to look for an opportunity to take advantage of them. It is safe to say that a poor man has no friends. Even members of your own family might be trying to stay away from you because they are of the conviction that any contact you make with them is a window to seek financial assistance. In the end, you find yourself being alienated even by the people you hold dear. When people that are close to you don't want to be around you, you can guess what strangers would think about you. In conclusion, it is safe to say that money as well as other factors of physics makes the world spin on it axis.

The power and reach that money possesses can never be overemphasized. No matter the situation you might find yourself in, there is always a way out. It does not matter how difficult the task might seem. The most important thing is to identify the problem and attempt to go about solving it in the right way. If you encounter a task that no one can solve, then it becomes an impossibility. "May God grant me the serenity to accept the things I cannot change; the courage to change the things I can and the wisdom to know the difference."

There are those problems that money cannot solve especially those related to health and death and there are problems that money can solve ranging from paying a parking ticket to buying a drug for headache. The first thing to consider when you find yourself in a complex situation is try to determine if you have the capacity to solve the problem. Then proceed to determining if the problem if something that money can solve. If this condition is satisfied, then you can go ahead to check what you have before jumping to spend your hard-earned money. The solution might be long term or short term depending on the nature of the problem you encounter. Do not be quick to jump into conclusions.

Problems related to romance like marriage and relationships cannot be solved be solved by money irrespective of the amount you spend on them. There is no price for human emotions and happiness. World issues like disease, famine, wars and conflicts are way too complex to be solved by spending money on them. Behavioral problems like poor business or money management is a problem money cannot solve. You cannot spend money to cover your losses.

Emotional problems and other related problems like mid-life crisis cannot be solved financially.

Not all problems that money can solve should be solved with money. Trying to change bad grades by paying does not make you any intelligent, though it might guarantee a better certificate. It is like trying to fight drug addiction with more drugs or trying to stop wars by selling ammunition to both conflicting sides. Paying a fine for lateness or for breaking a rule is an undesirable expense.

Problems should serve as a wake-up call for us to go into action by trying to determine the cause of the problem and trying our best to avoid recurrence. If you try to stop a fire by ignoring it, it will end up burning everything you have. You should consider trying to get advice from someone. A fresh perspective is always a good idea because what we are seeing is never the whole picture. From that fresh perspective, you should make comparisons and draw conclusions.

You should be careful in choosing the right course of action because solving the problem the wrong way might worsen the situation by creating more problems. After analyzing the solutions then you can go ahead to solve the problem.

You should try as much as possible not to make the same mistakes that left you in the situation you found yourself in. Create an emergency budget to take care of such unforeseen circumstances but at the same time try to lead a lifestyle that won't require you making such unnecessary expenses. You have to try hard to identify the unnecessary products that eat away at your budget. Create a plan to pay off your debts as soon as possible or employ the services of a trusted expert. Learn from your mistakes.

Principle 6. Do not keep the money. If it is destined to leave, it will leave.

Money is not a very easy commodity to come by, which is why most people are reluctant when they find themselves in situations where they are required to part with what they have got. This might be as a result of an unpredictable economy which tends to affect decision making. People that have been in financial crisis are often skeptical to spend on things that are not part of the essentials for fear that it might come back to haunt them. Their first instinct is to hang on to the money and save up for a rainy day. This is a good idea but might not be the best course of action.

Money is always in constant flow. If you have the right attitude towards money, it will come to you. If you spend your cash carefully and on productive things, you will get back the value for your money. Trying to control the flow of the money you have at your disposal, by being frugal, does not guarantee financial security. It makes one miss out on the opportunities that life presents before us. You have to spend the money you have got to make more money.

One should apply wisdom and caution when they are dealing with money. The fact that money is in constant flow doesn't mean that you can escape the consequences of careless spending. You should remember to stay within your budget limit to avoid running into debt. Do not spend your money on things just because you feel the impulse to have them. Make sure they are really necessary and once the necessity is determined, you should not be reluctant to get them. Do not be reluctant to give yourself a nice treat once it is within your budget. Money is meant to help people get the best out of life and not the other way around.

Do not get attached. Money is a resource that can be restored. It is better to take care of time, health and strength.

The global system is structured in such a way that everything revolves around money, just like the sun in the solar system. People place a lot of value on money which might be mostly based on emotional attachment. According to popular belief, money is a commodity that can help you fulfill your needs. Money serves to enhance human emotion by driving us towards achieving our essential human needs. People tend to show-off their financial buoyancy to their neighbours as a way to make them feel they are living a better life. This might be a façade to cover up the real emotional problems they are facing. Riches cannot buy happiness.

As much as one might want to believe that money is the most important thing in life, it is unfortunately false. People are driven by love while money is all about math and numbers.

There are places the two intersect but human emotions and values should always take priority. What is the essence of being rich if it is just to cause harm to people around you? This defeats all the purposes of making money. No matter the amount of money you have, if you have a repulsive, arrogant or unreliable personality, people would not want to associate with you unless they are looking to take advantage of the riches you have got. If you have a disheveled look and have a wallet full of cash, people would barely take you serious. Some might even think that you stole the cash.

If you attach yourself to something fully, you would be left distraught when is taken away from you. This goes a long way to prove that love, satisfaction and contentment are the most important things in life. That is why you cry when you lose a loved one or feel upset when your favorite pet dies. It is the reason you feel bad when you see your fellow human suffering. Once you lose these qualities, you then become a robot. One can buy all the medicine in life but not health. You can buy a book but not knowledge and common sense. You can hire a clown but not laughter. All these qualities are things we acquire throughout our life on earth. They do not depend on the amount of money we have.

"What shall it profit a man if he gains the whole world and suffers the loss of his soul?"

Soul in this context might be used to represent the emotional, mental and psychological characteristics of any human being. Peace of mind, integrity, trust, happiness and quality time with family and friends are some of the things that might come under threat if you continue on your path to acquire wealth at all costs without considering the consequences. Mahatma Gandhi once said, "if you have a strong vision of doing something good to the society, I tell you resources will come all by itself. Nature will start helping you". If you are ready to do good in the society, the resources would make their way to you. Look at the children in the playground, all they care about is to have fun and enjoy the simple things in life. Yet they always find a way to stay happy and content despite the fact that they don't have the resources to buy the latest products in the market.

"Can you step back from you own mind and thus understand all things? Giving birth and nourishing, having without possessing, acting with no expectations, leading and not trying to control: this is the supreme virtue."

Lao Tzu

You need to understand that nothing lasts forever. People and things come and go at an indefinite time. You should cherish the moments of our life as they come instead of spending all your time trying to amass wealth which you might actually not get to spend. You have to make the best of the situation you find yourself in irrespective of where you are. If you take care of yourself, what is yours will surely come to you.

Principle 7. Money is an energy.

Money, just like time, is a form of exchange of energy and services from one form to another. Money itself is not an energy but is stirs up our inner feelings. The mere sight of the paper or metal, or the thought of the numbers can arouse emotions like joy or sorrow. This energy is what makes us anxious or relieved whenever we hear of economic changes like crashing of the stock market. This is the subconscious energy. A misuse of the energy generated can lead one into feeling a sense of guilt or greed. The physical and practical energy is the sum total of all the activities that involve direct contact with money. It involves the way we spend, the way we save and the things we invest in. These decisions are highly influenced by the subconscious energy.

The energy that comes about with coming in contact with money can lead us to success in all spheres of life if properly channeled. Success is when you achieve all your set out goals with consistency and ease. One should cultivate a healthy mindset and attitude to work. We should try to see money as a friend rather than a foe because it really affects the way we are going to treat it. You trust your friend and distrust your foe. If you trust money, you will be able to positively channel the energy you receive into your life to make you happy. Whereas if you do not trust money, you treat it with skepticism and in the end, you find yourself being stressed out and full of anxiety.

You have to be clear on your priorities and try as much as possible not to make wild guesses when it comes to financial issues. What the heart wants might not always be the same as what we really need. Our needs should take priority no matter the situation. Endeavour to make your life as simple as possible. There is no extra reward for complicating issues for yourself. Our attitude towards money goes a long way to explain what you value the most and in extension – what you are all about. Time management is also a way of getting the best out of the energy being transferred. If you manage your time well, it will help you to take good care of your finances. Money and time are related in the sense that a proper management of your time would ensure maximum productivity and financial security.

About author

Daniel P. Richardson

Businessman, founder and owner of the real estate corporation, a highly qualified specialist in the field of running own business, money management, coach, start-ups consultant, and investor.

Author of books on money management, personal finance, self-development, start-ups and motivational.

Happy family man, father of three children.

Thank you for buying my book! I hope you get a lot of good stuff out of it.

I wanted to show my appreciation that you support my work so I've put together a free gift for you.

GET YOUR GIFT!

Just visit the link above to download it now.

I know you will love this gift.

Thanks readers for reviewing my book!

www.ingramcontent.com/pod-product-compliance
Lightning Source LLC
Chambersburg PA
CBHW061229180526
45170CB00003B/1223